MY FIRST EASY
Guitar Tablature Book

MW00523250

Elementary - Late Elementary

by Philip Groeber

CONTENTS

About This Book

What's Up With This TAB?

This is the book that you have been looking for, an easy to play, systematic way to help you learn all about guitar tablature. Although it may seem complex, learning tablature is quite simple, and you will find yourself reading guitar TAB in no time.

TAB uses an informal approach to playing music on your guitar. Learning to read music on the traditional 5-line staff (standard notation) is a more thorough approach to learning and appreciating music, but does take considerable more time and effort on the part of the student. TAB is a very effective way to learn new music quickly, even if you can't read music. If you already have music-reading skills, TAB will also be very helpful to you, especially when playing in higher positions.

The information in this book is intended for the guitar student who has some experience playing notes, riffs, or chords. This book is a superb supplement to any Grade 1 guitar method for students taking private or group lessons and also for the student who is teaching themselves to play guitar and wants to understand music written specifically for the guitar.

The use of TAB in this book allows the author to introduce many guitar playing tips that are not often included in most beginning guitar methods. Look for these tips throughout the book.

Chord names and frames are also provided. The voicings are kept in basic forms since this is a book written for solo (melody) performance and not chord instruction. If the student can play more advanced chords, they are encouraged to do so.

The performance tracks are intended to allow the student to hear how the song goes to ensure that they are playing the correct notes at the correct times. Playing along with the tracks is encouraged.

Here is an example of what guitar tablature looked like hundreds of years ago.

Tablature 101

Read Me

Once you realize that TAB is just a graphic look at the neck of your guitar, the concept of TAB becomes apparent. There are six horizontal lines grouped together, and each one of them represents a guitar string. The top line indicates the 1st string of the guitar (the skinniest one), and the bottom line represents the 6th string (the thickest one). You will then probably notice that there are numbers centered on some of the strings. These numbers indicate the fret on which you place your fingers.

In the example below, the stacked letters TAB indicates that this is a TAB staff. The number 3 (meaning 3rd fret) and the number 0 (meaning open string) are placed on the first string. No other strings and only these two notes are to be played. The vertical lines descending from the numbers are the stems of **quarter notes** (one beat each).

The next example show a little more movement using **eighth notes** with beams (1/2 beat each).

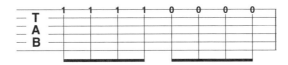

When several numbers are stacked on top of each other you will be playing a **chord**. A chord will use anywhere between 3 and 6 strings. Below is an Em chord played as **half notes**.

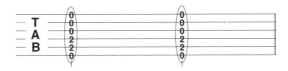

This book will use a TAB staff that shows you two things, the fret on which to play, and the rhythm of the note (how long to hold the note). This form of TAB is closely related to the five-line staff. However, when using TAB from the internet, referred to as ASCII TAB, you will usually find TAB numbers *without any indication of the rhythm*. Turn to page 28 to learn more about ASCII TAB.

Below is an example of the TAB format we will use throughout most of this book including labels for the musical terms that you need to know. It is a combination of a 5-line staff (standard notation) and a 6-line TAB staff. This format will be referred to as Published TAB.

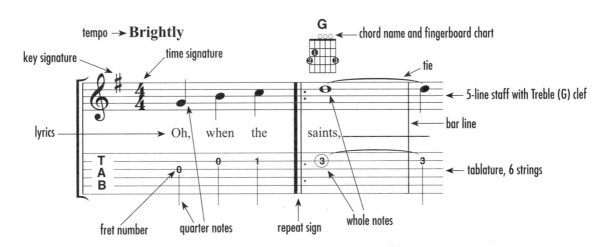

Time to Play!

Open Strings with Quarter Notes

- Let's begin by using only one line of the tablature staff.

- The music below only uses the TAB number 0, indicating the open string (no left-hand fingers).

- This gives you more time to concentrate on WHEN to play the open string using quarter notes.

- Place your pick on the first (the skinniest) string, ready to strum down (∎), towards the floor.
  Then play a few notes on the first string open. Look at your right hand as you play.
  Place your left hand on the guitar neck for balance. Do not let any part of your left-hand touch the open strings.

QUARTER NOTES ON THE FIRST STRING (E) Track 1 can also be used as a source for tuning.

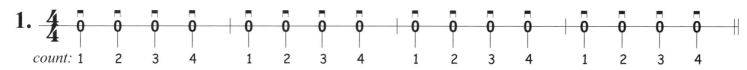

Now, think about WHEN you play the note. Keep a steady beat as you play, every one of these quarter notes needs to be played evenly, not too fast, not to slow. Every quarter note receives the same beat. Think of the ticking of a clock or the beat of your pulse. Music needs this steady pulse. Counting four beats a measure as indicated below the notes is very useful to help you play with a steady pulse. The top number of the **time signature** tells you how many beats are in a measure.

QUARTER NOTES ON THE SECOND STRING (B)

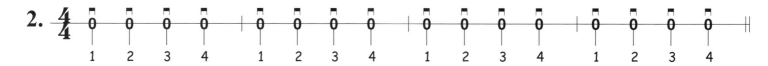

Using the same one-line TAB staff, move your right hand up to the second string (B) and look at your hand as you begin to play. Watch out! It is very easy to accidentally play the first string so be careful!

QUARTER NOTES ON THE THIRD THROUGH SIXTH STRINGS

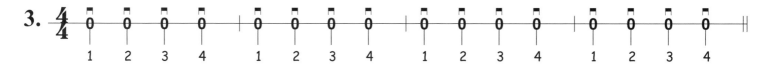

Now play the remaining four strings as open strings. You will find that the thicker the string, the lower the sound.

Concentrate on being accurate, don't worry about how fast you play. Always remember to keep a steady pulse with your quarter notes!

TIP FOR MUSICIANSHIP
The concept of playing with a steady pulse is *very* important!

Open Strings with Eighth Notes

- Two eighth notes receive one beat, so they are played a little faster than quarter notes.
  (A single eighth note receives 1/2 beat.)
  Count aloud saying: *1 and 2 and 3 and 4 and*, etc.

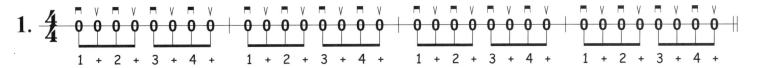

- Place your pick on any string, and strum down (⊓) and up (v) as shown below.

2 EIGHTH NOTES ON THE FIRST STRING

1.

TIP FOR MUSICIANSHIP

1) It is important to get comfortable playing notes on all six strings!
2) Sometimes play loud, other times soft.

Adding the Left Hand

- Follow the left-hand fingering as indicated: open string, 1st finger, third finger.

- Place your left-hand fingers directly behind the fret to help you create a clear sound.

- The TAB numbers we will be using are: 0 = open string, 3 = third fret, 5 = 5th fret.

- Concentrate on playing with a steady pulse!

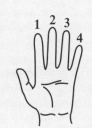

MIXING UP QUARTER NOTES AND EIGHTH NOTES ON THE FIRST STRING

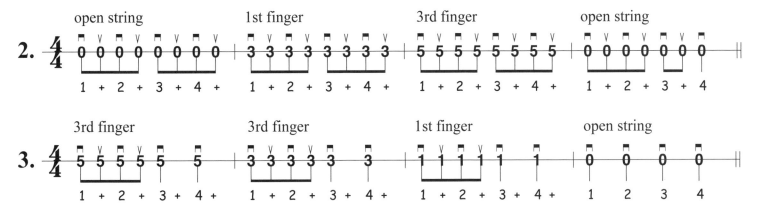

Be sure you can play Exercises 2 and 3 accurately before turning the page.
Carefully listen to the audio tracks to be sure you are playing correctly.
Once your are comfortable playing eighth notes on the first string, play this page on all strings.

PRE-READING TAB

Songs on One String

- The following songs use TAB numbers only on one string.

- Use your first finger for fret 3 and your third finger for fret 5.

- Songs that can be played on only one string will make your left hand move around a lot. Play as smoothly and connected as possible.

- Then, when you are comfortable, play the songs on any other string. Follow the same TAB numbers and finger numbers.

- Teacher Note: The chord names on pages 6 thru 9 only apply when the student is playing on the 1st or 6th strings.

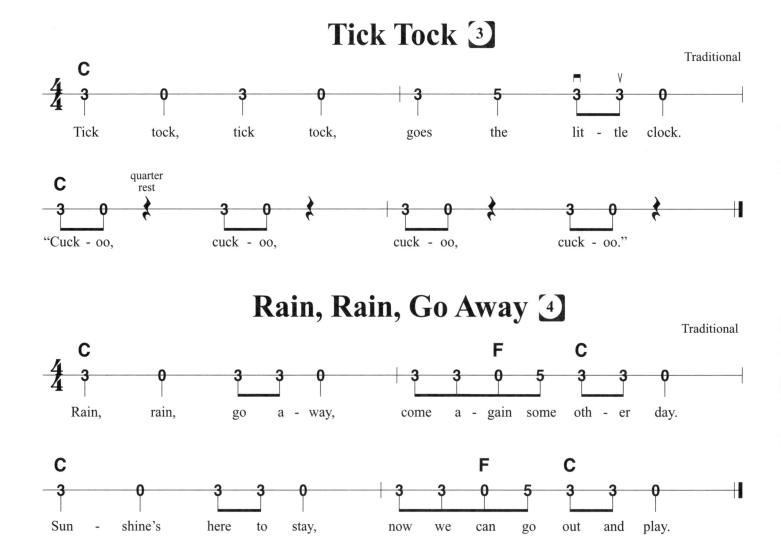

Tick Tock 3

Traditional

Tick tock, tick tock, goes the lit - tle clock.

"Cuck - oo, cuck - oo, cuck - oo, cuck - oo."

Rain, Rain, Go Away 4

Traditional

Rain, rain, go a - way, come a - gain some oth - er day.

Sun - shine's here to stay, now we can go out and play.

TIP FOR MUSICIANSHIP

A rest indicates a period of silence. You may have to stop the string from vibrating with either hand.

Lucy Locket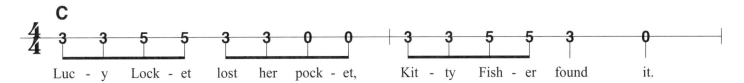

Traditional

C

4/4 | 3 3 5 5 | 3 3 0 0 | 3 3 5 5 | 3 0 |

Luc - y Lock - et lost her pock - et, Kit - ty Fish - er found it.

C

| 3 3 5 5 | 3 3 0 0 | 3 3 5 5 | 3 0 |

Not a pen - ny was there in it, on - ly rib - bon on it.

 **GUITAR TIP**

GUIDE FINGERS

- *Hot Cross Buns* uses a technique called a **Guide Finger**. When using the same left-hand finger for two or more consecutive notes on the same string, gently glide from one note to the next without lifting your finger off the string. This technique makes moving from one note to another much easier, and the notes will be smoothly connected.

- In *Hot Cross Buns* play the note on the 7th fret with your third finger. When moving the third finger down to the next note on the 5th fret, slightly release your finger pressure and glide down to the fifth fret. Use the same technique when moving higher from the 5th fret to the 7th fret.

Hot Cross Buns

Traditional

G   **D**   **G**   **D**   **G**

3 — guide — 3

4/4 | 7   5   ③ | 7   5   ③ |

Hot cross buns, hot cross buns,

G   **D**   **G** **D** **G**

| 3 3 3 3 | 5 5 5 5 | 7   5   ③ |

one a pen - ny, two a pen - ny, hot cross buns!

┌─────────────────────────────┐
│ **TIP FOR MUSICIANSHIP** │
│ A half notes receive two beats.   ③ │
└─────────────────────────────┘

8

Playing on Higher Frets

- The left-hand fingering will be indicated above the fret number.

- Whenever possible use the Guide Finger technique from page 7. Smoothly connect *all* of the notes.

- The songs on pages 8 and 9 can be played on any of the six strings. Because the strings vary in thickness, songs sound a little different on various strings. In addition, every string has a different name (**pitch**). Pick the string that you like the best for each song. For example, the Halloween song, *Ghostess are the Mostess!* sounds cool when played on the sixth string!

- NOTE: The chord names only apply when the melody is played on the 1st or 6th string.

Ghostess are the Mostess! ⑦

Philip Groeber

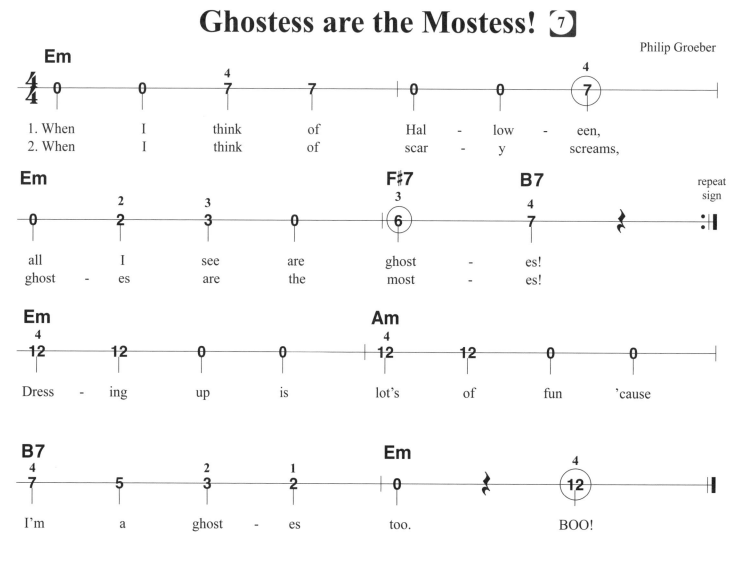

 **GUITAR TIP** The indicated left-hand fingering is the ideal way to play these songs. However, if the fingering gets in the way of your progress, any left-hand finger may be used. Starting on page 12 the fingering indications are very important and need to be followed.

There are other concepts being learned at this time that are more important than correct fingering.

1) Learning to play songs using tablature
2) Playing the correct note on the correct fret with a pleasing sound
3) Playing with a steady pulse
4) Having fun playing music on your guitar!

Solfa-Round 8

Traditional

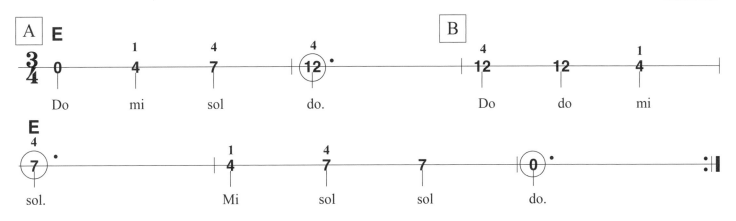

Solfa-Round is written in a musical style called a **round**. To perform as a round, you need at least two players. Player 1 begins as usual at letter A. Player 2 begins from the beginning of the song (A) as Player 1 gets to B. Play as long as you wish. If Player 2 ends up playing the last two measures by themselves, then everything worked out perfectly!

Twinkle, Twinkle 9

Traditional

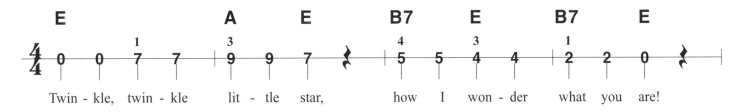

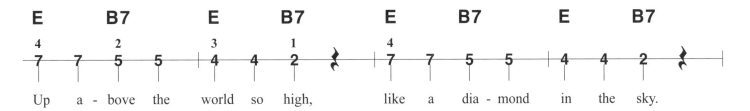

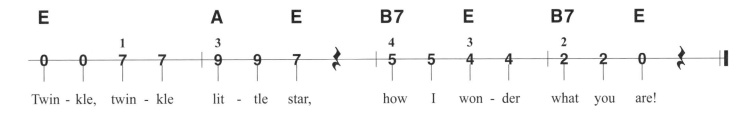

Note to the Teacher

Pages 8-11 use a innovative guitar instruction technique that encourages a student to play numerous notes on a single string as opposed to learning only two or three notes. The advantages for the student are: being able to concentrate on maintaining a steady beat by using mostly quarter notes, work on obtaining a clear tone, improving the coordination of both hands to simultaneously play on the same string, and experiencing playing the higher pitches on a guitar where the frets are closer together. In addition, students generally feel empowered by playing high on the neck in their beginning stages of study.

Songs on Two Strings

- The TAB staff now has TWO lines showing both the first string E and the second string B.

- Remember BOTH of your hands will be moving back and forth from one string to another.

- The left-hand fingering is indicated above the fret number.

Space Cadets 🔟

Philip Groeber

Play four times

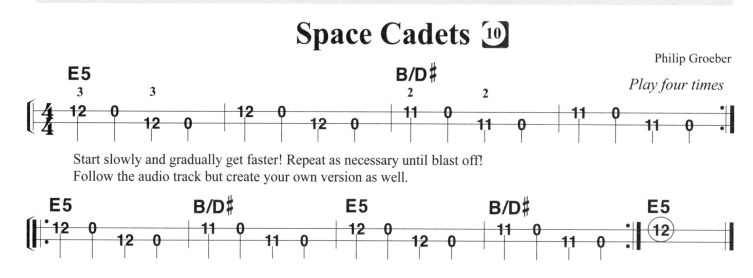

Start slowly and gradually get faster! Repeat as necessary until blast off!
Follow the audio track but create your own version as well.

Au Clair de la Lune ⑪

Traditional

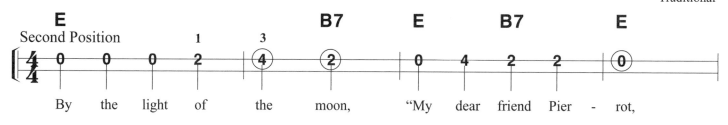

By the light of the moon, "My dear friend Pier - rot,

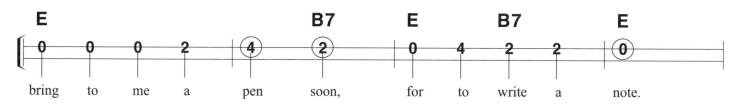

bring to me a pen soon, for to write a note.

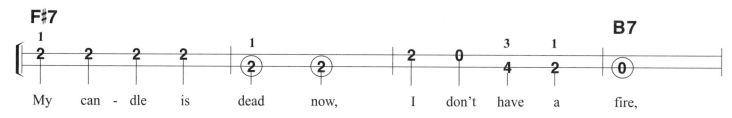

My can - dle is dead now, I don't have a fire,

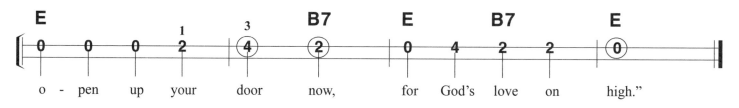

o - pen up your door now, for God's love on high."

 **GUITAR TIP** *Au Clair de la Lune* is played in **Second Position**. Keep your 1st finger on the second fret and your 3rd finger on the fourth fret.

Ring Around the Rosy 12

Traditional

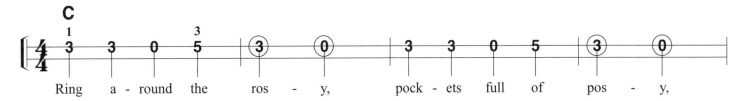

Ring a - round the ros - y, pock - ets full of pos - y,

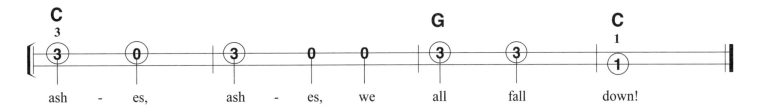

ash - es, ash - es, we all fall down!

Jingle Bells 13

James Pierpont

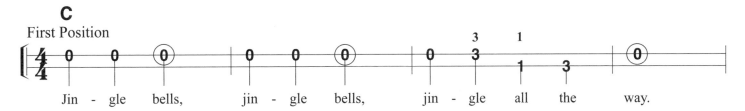

Jin - gle bells, jin - gle bells, jin - gle all the way.

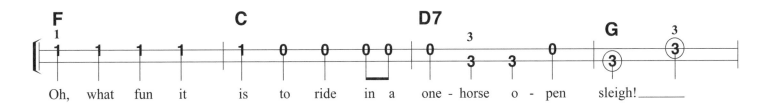

Oh, what fun it is to ride in a one - horse o - pen sleigh!_____

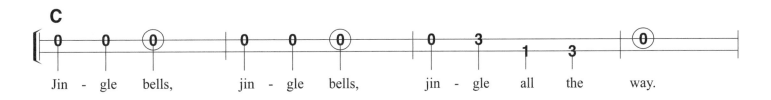

Jin - gle bells, jin - gle bells, jin - gle all the way.

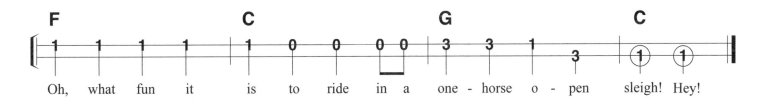

Oh, what fun it is to ride in a one - horse o - pen sleigh! Hey!

GUITAR TIP *Jingle Bells* is played in **First Position**. The left-hand finger number will be the same as the TAB number.

COMPLETE TAB WITH THE FIVE-LINE STAFF

- A five-line music staff will now appear above the tablature, creating what is referred to as Published TAB. The Published TAB staff below clearly presents the notes of strings 1, 2, and 3 in **First Position**.

- When playing in First Position, the left-hand finger number will match the TAB number. Most of the pieces in the rest of this book will be in First Position. Any position other than First Position will be indicated at the beginning of the song. Position indications only apply to playing melody.

- The note A on the fifth fret of the first string will be played with the 4th finger.

- Your left hand will not be moving from lower to higher frets as often, but will now be moving from string to string.

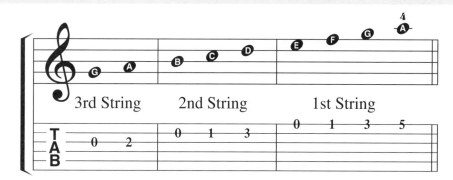

Notes on the First and Second Strings

Some Folks Do 14

Stephen Foster

 **GUITAR TIP** To see the BIG PICTURE, check out the two guitar charts on the inside back cover.

Mary Ann 15

Caribbean Folksong

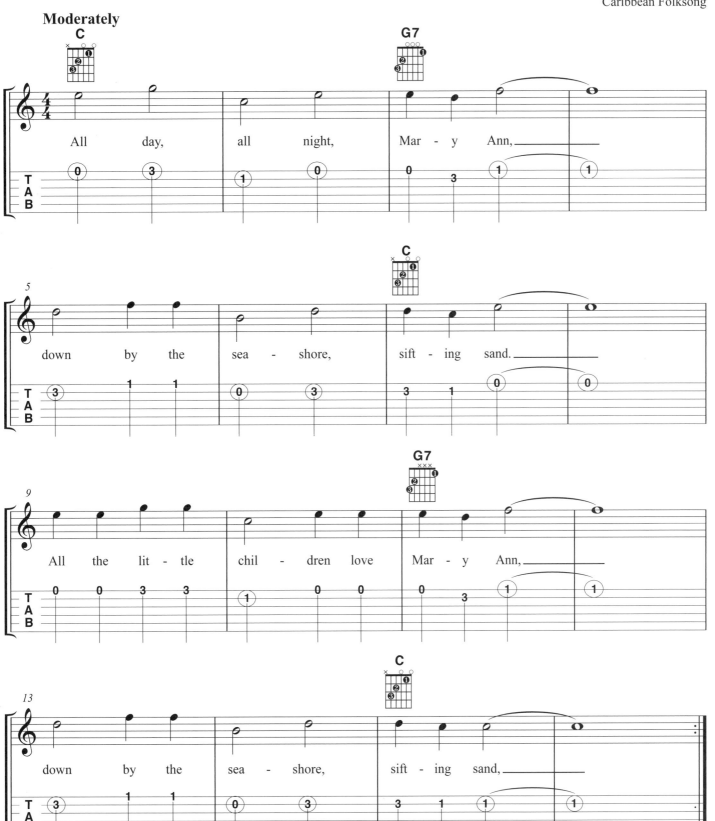

TIP FOR MUSICIANSHIP

Preapare yourself for future music-reading opportunities by using this book in three different ways:
1) Play the songs using only the TAB staff
2) Play the songs using only the five-line staff
3) Strum the chords

Notes on the Third String

Oh, When the Saints Go Marching In

American Folksong

 **HISTORY** | Jazz trumpet player Louis Armstrong made the first recording of "Saints" in 1938.

Bingo 17

Traditional

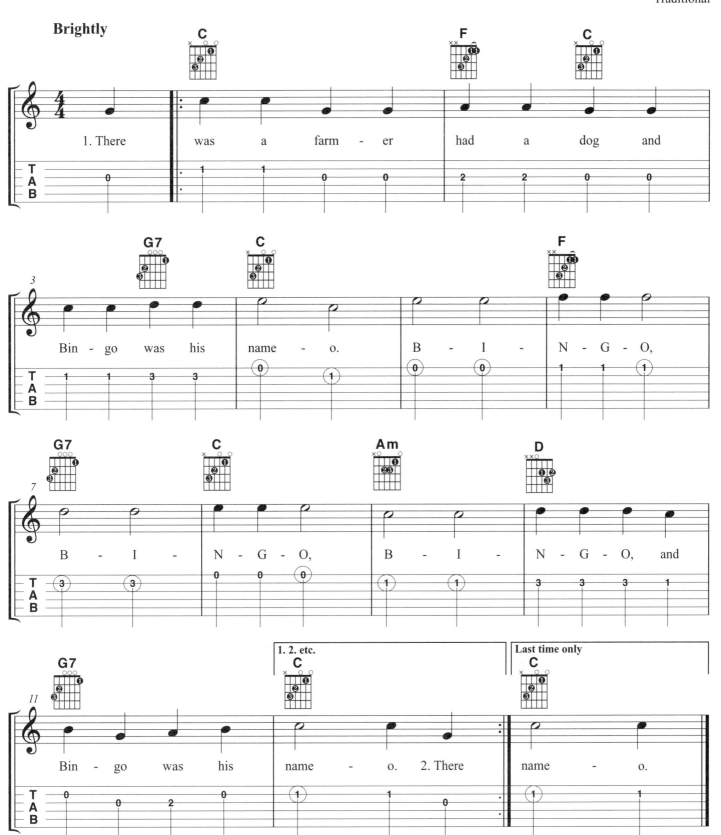

On succeeding verses, clap for one or more letters when spelling *Bingo*.

2nd verse:	clap	I	N	G	O
3rd verse:	clap	clap	N	G	O
4th verse:	clap	clap	clap	G	O
5th verse:	clap	clap	clap	clap	O
6th verse:	clap	clap	clap	clap	clap

Aura Lee 18

Traditional

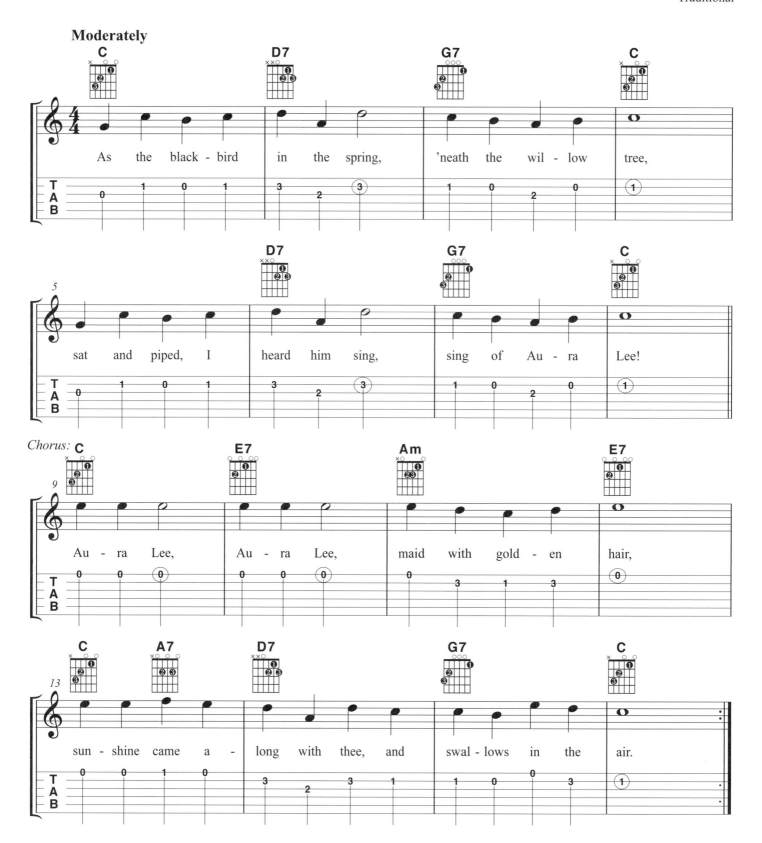

 Elvis Presley (The "King of Rock and Roll") heard the song *Aura Lee* and greatly admired the melody. He later added his own lyrics, made a recording, and renamed the song *Love Me Tender.*

Scarborough Fair 🔟

Traditional English

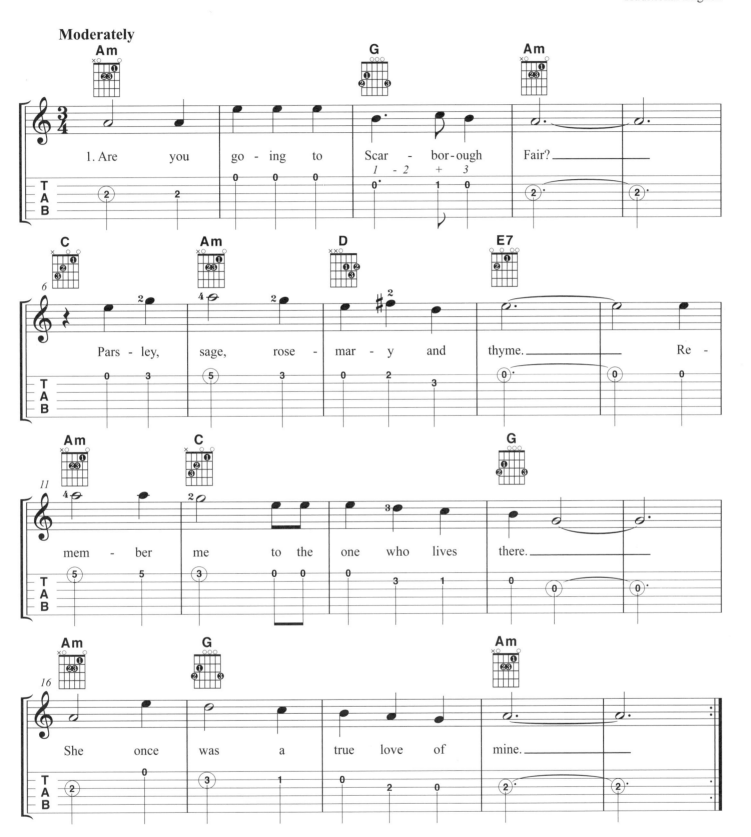

2. Tell her to make me a cambric shirt,
   parsley, sage, rosemary, and thyme;
   Sewn without seams or fine needlework,
   if she would be a true love of mine.

3. Tell her to wash it in yonder well,
   parsley, sage, rosemary, and thyme;
   Where never spring water or rain ever fell,
   and she shall be a true love of mine.

4. Tell her to dry it on yonder thorn,
   parsley, sage, rosemary, and thyme;
   Which never bore blossom since Adam was born,
   then she shall be a true love of mine.

Notes on the Fourth String

Amazing Grace

John Newton

TIP FOR MUSICIANSHIP

An **octave** is a musical term for two notes with the same name but 12 frets apart. For example you know the E on the open first string and now you have learned a lower-pitched E on the 2nd fret of the 4th string. Also, the 12th fret is always one octave higher than the open string.

Romanza 21

Traditional

Good Morning to You 22

Traditional Melody

Good morn-ing to you; And how do you do? Please en-

joy_____ your eve-ning; Good morn-ing to you!

Sing the lyrics to *Happy Birthday* when playing the melody or strumming the chords!

Chords in TAB

Spanish Strum 23

Traditional

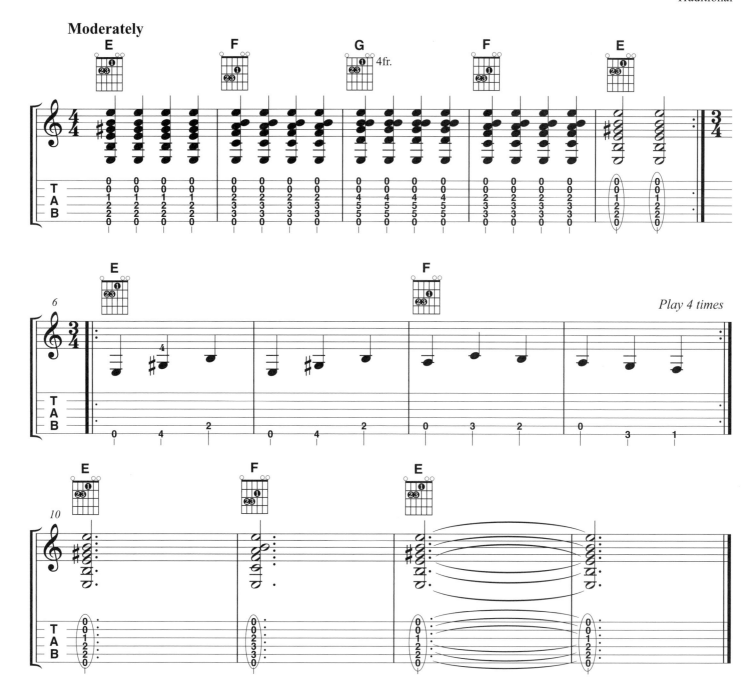

![TAB TIP]

Although the music looks intimidating at first glance, using the tablature will help you learn this famous guitar chord progression easily!

The F and G are specialized chords that only *approximate* the harmony. Measures 1-5 use the E chord fingering shape in three different positions.

Special Ending Rapidly strum with down and up strokes on the E chord in measures 12-13. Listen to Track 23.

Pachelbel Canon 24

Johann Pachelbel

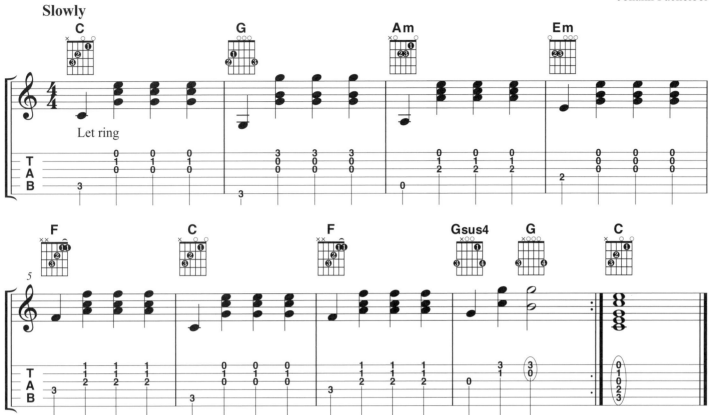

Hold the entire chord down with your fret hand and let your pick hand play the indicated strings. The fingering for some chords may be a little different. Be sure to follow the indicated fingering for the G chord in measure 8 of *Pachelbel Canon*.

The Four Chords 25

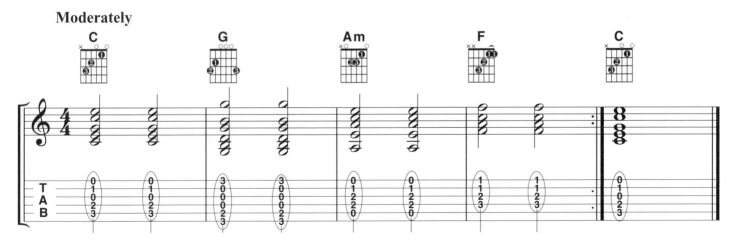

CREATIVITY

This chord progression is very common; in fact these four chords are used in hundreds of songs. On the internet these chords are referred to as "The Four Chords." Check it out.

Have fun with this chord progression and make up your own songs. Hum a melody that fits the chords and you will hear a really nice tune. You don't have to use the chords in the exact order they are presented here. You can "Let it Be" or "Let it Go."

Notes on the Fifth String

C Major Scale

Memorize!

Scales are very important to learn! Almost all songs are based on scales.
Practice this scale at least one minute each day. Sometimes play loudly, sometimes softly.

Latvian Lullaby

Traditional

Lul - a by, my ba - by,____ soft - ly

sleeps the child.____ Sis - ter rocks you

gent - ly,____ she is soft and mild.

TAB TIP

1) Look for TAB numbers that are in consecutive order, 0 2 3; 2 3 4; 3 2 1, etc. This tells you that the notes are in alphabetical order and a part of a scale.
2) Many songs use repeated numbers (notes). See *Ridin' That Train* on page 23 as an example.
3) When the same number appears on adjacent strings use the same finger to move over to the new note.

Volga Boatmen 28

Russian Folksong

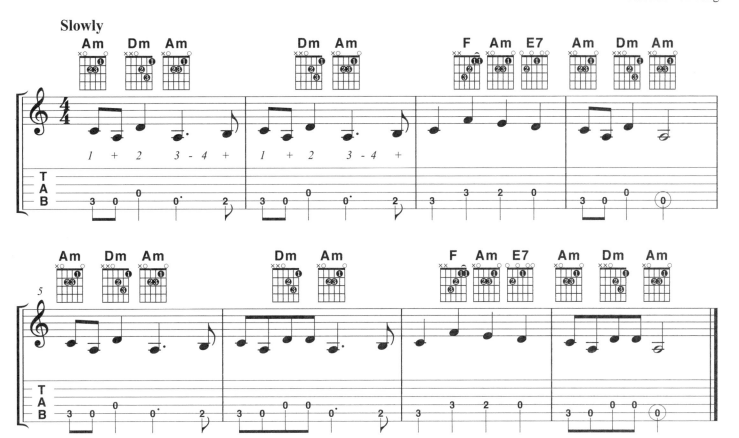

Ridin' That Train 29

Philip Groeber

 **GUITAR TIP** Chords with the suffix 5 indicates **Power Chords**. For example, an A5 chord contains only notes A and E, a D5 chord contains only notes D and A, and an E5 chord contains only notes E and B.

Guitar Techniques: Hammer-on, Pull-off, Slide, and Vibrato

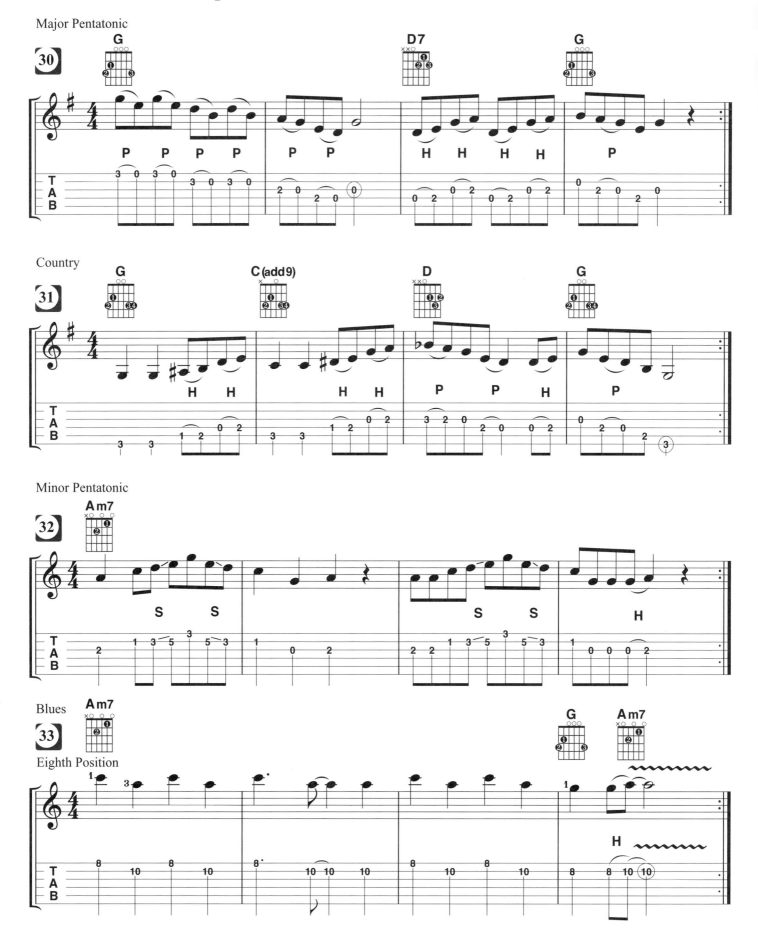

GUITAR TIP

Use these two steps to help you learn new music that uses new notes or techniques that are unfamiliar to you.

1) Concentrate on playing the correct notes and rhythm (pulse).
2) Gradually add the new techniques. Work on small sections at first, maybe a measure at a time.

THE A MINOR PENTATONIC SCALE

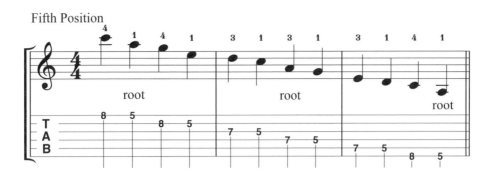

The A Minor Pentatonic Blues 34

Moderately fast

Philip Groeber

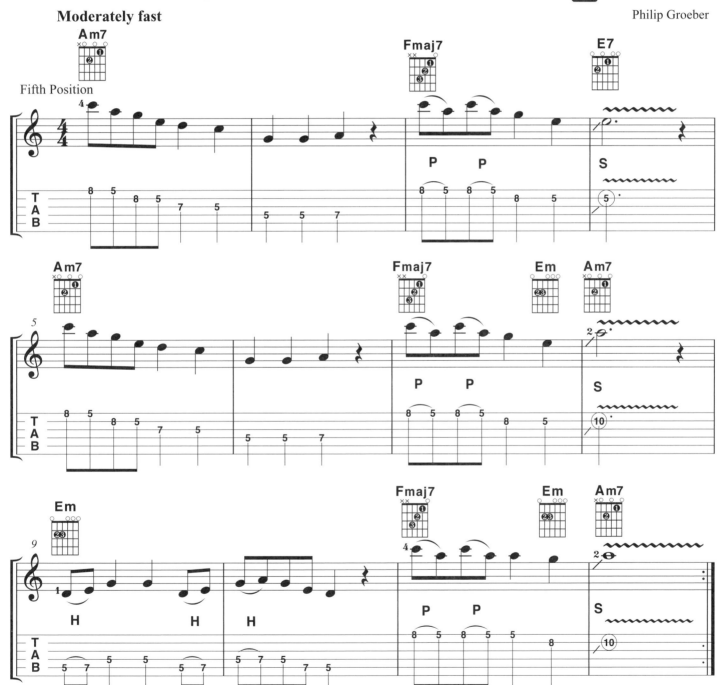

CREATIVITY

The A minor pentatonic scale in Fifth Position does not contain any open strings, so it is movable! For example, if you move the pattern down to Third Position, you are now playing a G minor pentatonic scale.

Notes on the Sixth String

G Major Scale 35

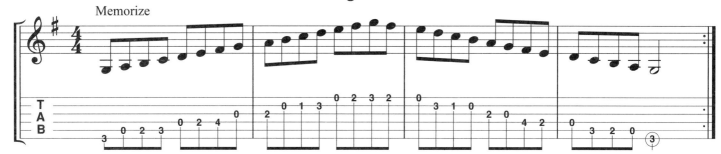

In the Key of G all the F notes will be played as sharps (♯).
Practice this scale at least one minute each day. Sometimes play loudly, sometimes softly.

TIP FOR MUSICIANSHIP

Look for notes in the 5-line staff that are in line-space order.
This tells you that the notes are in alphabetical order and are a part of a scale.

Chicago Blues 36

Philip Groeber

G Boogie 🎵37

Philip Groeber

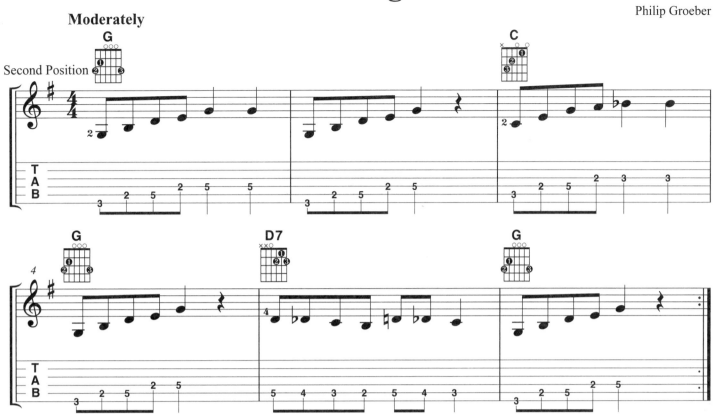

In the Hall of the Mountain King 🎵38

Edvard Grieg

INTERNET (ASCII) TABLATURE

- You may have noticed that tablature on the internet has a different appearance.

- Most tablature sites use ASCII TAB, which is easy to create and post on the internet.

- ASCII TAB is very basic and does not offer much more information than the location of a note on a string and fret. There is usually no indication of rhythm, chord names, or other music symbols. In addition, many of the ASCII TAB examples are even incorrect! Just because you use TAB found on the internet does not mean that is it always going to have the right information. Be prepared to fix or change incorrect numbers, chords, etc. Despite all of this, ASCII TAB *can be very helpful* when learning a new song.

- Here are several ASCII TAB examples to help make sense of tablature found on the internet.

EXAMPLE 1 [39]

Below are the first 8 measures of *Ode to Joy* by Beethoven.

The melody is probably familiar to you and is pretty easy to play. Most of the notes are quarter notes (1 beat each), and the longer note values have a little extra space after them. This is the beauty of tablature, when you already know the melody a new song can be learned in a short amount of time. Notice that there is no mention of time signatures, quarter notes, measures, ties, fingering, etc.

ODE TO JOY - BEETHOVEN

Tabbed by: PG

```
E|-0-0-1-3-|-3-1-0---|-------0-|-0-------|-0-0-1-3-|-3-1-0---|-------0-|---------|
B|---------|-------3-|-1-1-3---|---3-3---|---------|-------3-|-1-1-3---|-3-1-1---|
G|---------|---------|---------|---------|---------|---------|---------|---------|
D|---------|---------|---------|---------|---------|---------|---------|---------|
A|---------|---------|---------|---------|---------|---------|---------|---------|
E|---------|---------|---------|---------|---------|---------|---------|---------|
```

EXAMPLE 2 [40]

Example 2 has more movement from string to string. When there are eight equally-spaced tab numbers in a measure you can assume they are eighth notes (1/2 beat each).

Since you haven't heard this song before, you have to hope that the TAB is accurate and easy to read. Without bar lines it is a little more difficult to keep track of where you are.

BOOGIE BLUES - PG

Tabbed by: PG

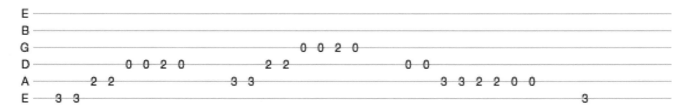

EXAMPLE 3 [41]

Example 3 has you playing on higher frets. Rarely are finger numbers indicated in ASCII TAB. Hint: Begin in Fifth Position; 1st finger on the 5th fret, second finger on the 6th fret, etc. *It's All Right* uses only three chords: A, D, and E. Can you identify where the chord changes occur?

IT'S ALL RIGHT - PG

TABBED BY: PG

```
E|-------------------------------------------------------------------------------
B|-------------------------------------------------------------------------------
G|---------------------------------5-5-7-7----------7-7-9-9-----------------------
D|-----------5-5-7-7-------7-7------------------9-9---------------5-5-7-7----------
A|------7-7----------------5-5------------7-7---------------------7-7--------------
E|---5-5--------------------------------------------5-5----------------5-----------
```

To help you determine which left-hand position is best for learning a riff or short example in ASCII TAB, look for the *lowest fret number*. This number will usually indicate the position you need to use. With this in mind, which left-hand position will you use for the last five notes in Example 4 below, *Where're You Going*? _____

EXAMPLE 4 [42]

Example 4 primarily uses chords. There may or may not be chord names indicated. Sometimes the chord names appear only on the first entry of the chord. You may have to recognize the rest of the chords by the fret indications.

WHERE'RE YOU GOING? - PG

TABBED BY: PG

```
        C     G     D     A     E
E|-0----3-----2-----0-----0-------------------
B|-1----0-----3-----2-----0-------------------
G|-0----0-----2-----2-----1-------------------
D|-2----0-----0-----2-----2-------------5-----
A|-3----2-----------0-----2------5-------7--
E|-0----3-----------------0----7----7-------
```

Some TABs list chords and their voicings using fret numbers starting with the 1st string like the examples below.

```
C - 0 1 0 2 3        G - 3 0 0 0 2 3        D - 2 3 2 0

A - 0 2 2 2 0        E - 0 0 1 2 2 0        F - 1 1 2 3

Bb - 6 6 7 8         Eb - 3 4 3 5          Ab - 4 4 5 6
```

Compare these chord examples to the chords in the TAB of *Where're You Going?* above.

Below are several snippets of ASCII TAB that are transcribed into Published TAB.

ASCII TAB   Published TAB

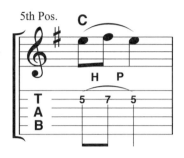

combination of a hammer-on and a pull-off

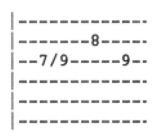
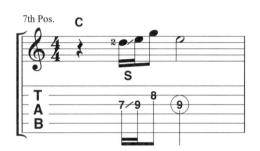

a sixteenth-note slide at a slow tempo

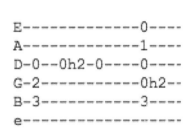
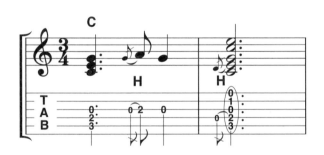

chord example with hammer-ons
(notice the incorrect labeling of the strings in the ASCII TAB example)

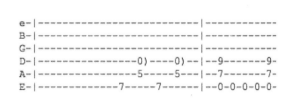
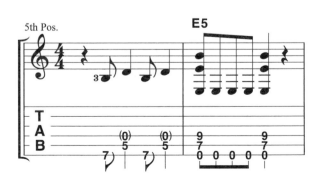

the fourth string open D is an optional note
(compare the various graphic styles of ASCII TAB)

EXAMPLE 6

Putting It All Together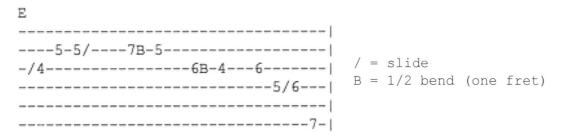

Here are two TAB versions of the same music. Both examples sound the same.

ASCII TAB

```
E
-------------------------------------|
----5-5/----7B-5---------------------|
-/4-----------------6B-4---6----------|      / = slide
------------------------------5/6----|       B = 1/2 bend (one fret)
-------------------------------------|
------------------------------7-|
```

Published TAB

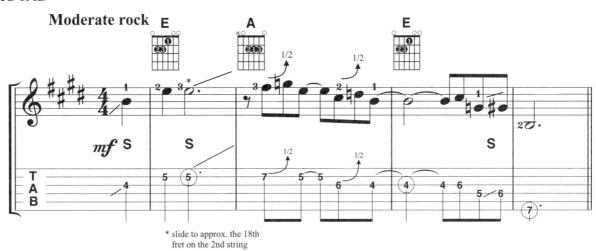

* slide to approx. the 18th
fret on the 2nd string

Let's compare both of the TAB versions above:	ASCII	Published TAB
1) Does it look intimidating?	a little	yes
2) Is there enough information for an accurate performance if the performer is very familiar with the recording?	yes	yes
3) Is there enough information for an accurate performance if the performer is not familiar with the recording?	no	yes
4) Does the performer need specialized note-reading skills?	no	yes
5) Does the performer need specialized guitar skills?	yes	yes

THE TAB WRAP UP

ASCII TAB is very helpful when the performer is familiar with the recording. However, some information may be missing or at least unclear.

Published TAB is so accurate that even a person unfamiliar with the recording can still reproduce the intent of the composer *if they are skilled in reading music.*

Glossary

accidentals	sharps (♯) raise a note 1 fret; flats (♭) lower a note 1 fret; naturals (♮) cancel sharps and flats
alternate picking	using downstrokes (⊓) and upstrokes (∨)
bend	a guitar technique where a left-hand finger pushes (bends) a string to the side to achieve a higher pitch. ASCII TAB usually uses the letter "B" to indicate a bend, Published TAB uses fractions along with an arrow: 1/4 a slight bend; 1/2 a half-step bend (one fret); 1 a whole-step bend (two frets).
fermata (⌢)	holding a note longer than its regular value
First Position	left-hand position where the finger numbers match the fret numbers
guide fingers	keeping a left-hand finger in contact with the string while moving to a different fret on the same string
hammer-on (H)	a guitar technique where a left-hand finger plays a note and then *hammers down* on another fret to sound the next note. The pick only plays the first note in a hammer-on. Hammer-ons are used on ascending notes.
harmony	notes played at the same time; chords
key signature	indicated at the beginning of every line of music. The key of C has no sharps or flats, the key of G has one sharp, F♯.
Let ring	holding notes down as long as you can in order to keep the strings vibrating
melody	the notes to a song; how the song goes
N.C. (No Chord)	all rhythm (chords) stops playing while the melody continues
note/rest values	denote how long to hold a note or rest: ♫ eighth notes (1/2 beat each), ♩ quarter note (1 beat), ♪ half note (2 beats), ♪. dotted half note (3 beats), o whole note (4 beats)
octave	notes with the same letter name but are 12 frets apart
pentatonic scale	a scale comprised of only 5 notes. For example an Am pentatonic scale uses only notes A, C, D, E, G.
pitch	the highness or lowness of a note
position playing	determined by the location of the first finger. Each consecutive finger plays the next consecutive fret.
pull-off (P)	a guitar technique where a left-hand finger *pulls off* of the string (toward the floor) to sound the next note. The pick only plays the first note in a pull-off. Pull-offs are used on descending notes.
rhythm	the timing of the music using various note values
slide (S)	a guitar technique where a left-hand finger slides from one note to another.
tempo	term that appears at the beginning of a song that lets a performer know how fast or slow the song is.
time signature	indicated at the beginning of every song. For example, 4/4 - the top 4 tells you there are four beats in a measure and the bottom 4 tells you that quarter notes receive one beat.
vibrato (〜〜)	a guitar technique where a left-hand finger gently and rapidly pushes the string back and forth to produce a pleasant sound. A good vibrato technique will allow the note to sustain for a longer time.